Start

86 Super-cute Toys and Accessories to Make Yourself

Felt Friends from Japan

Naomi Tabatha

Translated by Leeyong Soo

KODANSHA USA

Felt Friends from Japan

86 Super-cute Toys and Accessories to Make Yourself

Contents

Instructions

Tabletop Duo · · 14
Kenji the Cat and Mr. Sausage Dog

Forest Friends · · 16
Fumiko Fawn and Little Rabbit

Beret Buddies · · 18
Miki the Monkey and Pao the Elephant

Coin Purses and Card Cases
Cute 'n' Fun Accessories · · 20
Monkey Coin Purse • Panda Coin Purse • Elephant Coin Purse • Frog Coin Purse • Sausage Dog Pencil Case • Semicircle Coin Purses (Little Bird, Frog, Black Cat, Goldfish) • Chick Coin Purse • Little Bear Card Case • Card Case with Hearts

Flowers
Felt Flowers · · 22
--------- 12 Items
Fantastic Facts about Felt · · 23

Quick-tie Bags with Handles

Large Size · · 24

Medium Size · · 26

Small Size · · 27

Sweet Cell Phone Pouch · · 28

Felt Badges
Cute Felt Badges · · 30
-------- 25 Items

Handy Hints Before You Start · · 29

Afterword · · 64

Patterns

A Word of Welcome from Naomi Tabatha

When I was growing up, my mother was always stitching away at something. Seeing her at work on her creations was my introduction to the world of handicrafts.

Until recently, sewing was an everyday activity in most households. But somewhere along the way we stopped making and started buying. It seems to me that most people have forgotten how to make things, which is a shame, because there's nothing to compare with the sense of accomplishment that comes from creating something yourself, or the happy smile on a loved one's face when they receive a homemade gift you've spent hours making.

What I want to share with you through this book is the joy of

creating. I hope I can convey to you the warmth that comes from making something yourself with love and care.

All the toys and accessories in this book are made of felt and they can all be made by hand. If you think a project looks too challenging, just give it a try anyway and start sewing. As long as you take it one careful stitch at a time, you shouldn't have any problems, even if you're a beginner. Don't worry about making mistakes! Just have a go. I'm sure your creations will become your best friends.

Welcome to the cute and colorful world of handmade toys.

Naomi Tabatha

Mom's tail looks fun to chase!

Mom and Baby Kitty Cats

Pocket-sized Playmates
Best Buddies

instructions P. 32~35

These are so easy to make. Stitch them and stuff them and you're done.

Little Elephants

Here's cheers to having big ears!

Yellow Puppy Dog

Let's just the two of us go for a walk.

Orange Puppy Dog

Wanna know about a secret stash of carrots?

Boy Bunny

Girl Bunny

7

I'm ready for monkey business!

Cheeky Monkey

Shake paws!

Droopy-eared Dog

Pocket-sized Playmates

One Pattern, Eight Playmates

These little creatures all share the same pattern for their bodies, arms, and legs. Don't they just look like they'd love to hang out with you?

It's a purrfect time for adventure!

Little Black Cat

Does my head look big in this?

Mini Hana Hood

I just don't know what to do!

Bearly There

Wanna catch flies together?

Croaky Frog

instructions P. 36

Gotta get me some gum leaves!

Cuddly Koala

I see life in black and white . . .

Panda Pal

Brown Bear

This cute little guy is easy as pie to make, thanks to the simple pattern—all you need to do is join a few cylinders of felt together.

With me by your side, even sticky situations are easier to bear!

Brown
Bear

1. (Use whipstitch unless otherwise specified.) Following the diagrams below, stitch dart on snout. Stitch back of snout to snout. Insert stuffing and stitch snout to face. Sew eyebrows using straight stitch.

2. Stitch sides of head into a cylinder, then stitch front and back parts of head to either side of the cylinder, leaving a small opening in back of head. Insert stuffing until shape is firm, then stitch back of head closed.

3. Make ears and stitch to head.

4. Make body and stitch to head.

5. Make arms, legs, and tail and stitch to body.

6. Use glue to attach eyes, nose, and mouth.

Felt to Use

dark brown: 8" x 8", 2 sheets
beige: 4" x 4"
scraps of white, black, and red

● **pattern on p. 60**

side of head x 2

head x 2

body x 1

arm x 2

upper paw x 2

leg x 2

lower paw x 2

ear x 4

See P. 29 for stitches and other tips.

snout x 1

back of snout x 1

base x 1

eye x 2

pupil x 2

tail x 1

inner ear x 2

● nose x 1

mouth x 1

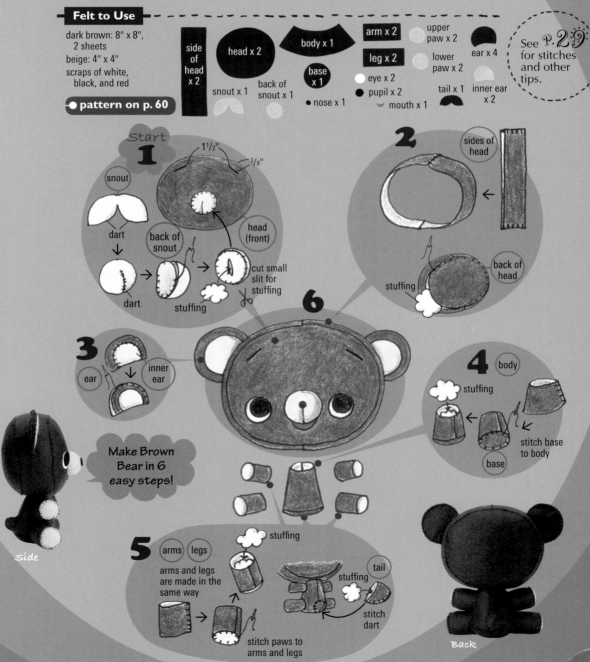

Start

1
1½"
3/8"
snout
dart
back of snout
dart
head (front)
cut small slit for stuffing
stuffing

2
sides of head
back of head
stuffing

3
ear
inner ear

6

Make Brown Bear in 6 easy steps!

4
body
stuffing
base
stitch base to body

Side

5
arms
legs
arms and legs are made in the same way
stitch paws to arms and legs
stuffing
stuffing
tail
stitch dart

Back

11

Brown Bear's Buddies

Trouser Bear, Rika the Rabbit, and Hana Hood are all variations of Brown Bear on page 10. Have fun experimenting!

instructions P. 38

I'm doing a dance in my fancy pants!

Trouser Bear

Rika the Rabbit

I'm Rika the Rabbit! I love the color pink that I'm made in. But check out the fancy pants on that bear!

Let's wash our hands and have a snack. I don't want to sound big-headed, but I'm pretty good at baking tasty cookies!

Hana Hood

Tabletop Duo

instructions P. 40 ★

Kenji
the Cat

"Hello, Mr. Sausage Dog!"
"Hello, Kenji the Cat!"
We always seem to meet at the same
time in the same place. A couple of
cute characters, out on the tabletop,
ready for fun.

Mr.
Sausage
Dog

I wish I could play more but I've got to go home.

Bye bye.

Fumiko Fawn

16

Forest Friends

instructions P.42

Bye bye.

Neither of us wants to be the first to leave! Tee hee!

Alright, on the count of three . . . One . . . two . . . three . . . See you tomorrow!

Little Rabbit

17

Miki the Monkey

18

Beret Buddies

It was a beautiful sunny day when I met Miki. It took a while for me to work up the courage to say hello to him, but it seems that he'd wanted to hang out with me all along. Our matching berets have magical powers. But nothing's more magical than making a new friend.

Pao the Elephant

instructions Ⓟ 44

19

Cute 'n' Fun Accessories

"Tee hee hee . . ." These characters seem to be having a giggle as they gossip. They all have such adorable expressions that you'll never want to part from them. Give them to your friends as presents and spread the smiles.

Monkey Coin Purse

Panda Coin Purse

Coins, pens and pencils, barrettes, jewelry . . . find a home for all your little things with these cute coin purses and cases.

Frog Coin Purse

Elephant Coin Purse

Sausage Dog Pencil Case

20

instructions P 46~49

Little Bird
Semicircle
Coin Purse

Use a snap fastener for these semicircle coin purses.

Frog Semicircle
Coin Purse

Black Cat
Semicircle
Coin Purse

Goldfish
Semicircle
Coin Purse

Naomi's business card
case is made of felt too! It's
sturdy and lasts a long time.

Little Bear
Card Case

Chick Coin Purse

Card Case
with Hearts

Felt Flowers

Don't throw away your leftover felt scraps! All you need to do to make these flowers is cut and layer the bits and pieces and fasten them together with a button or bead.

12 Items

Fantastic Facts
about Felt

Felt is colorful and warm, and it doesn't
fray, so there's no need to hem it. It's cheap
and can be bought in easy-to-use sizes,
so even beginners can have a go without
having to worry about making mistakes.
You don't have to use the same colors as in
the photos—why don't you experiment with
some of the many great shades available?

23

Quick-tie Bags with Handles

Large Size

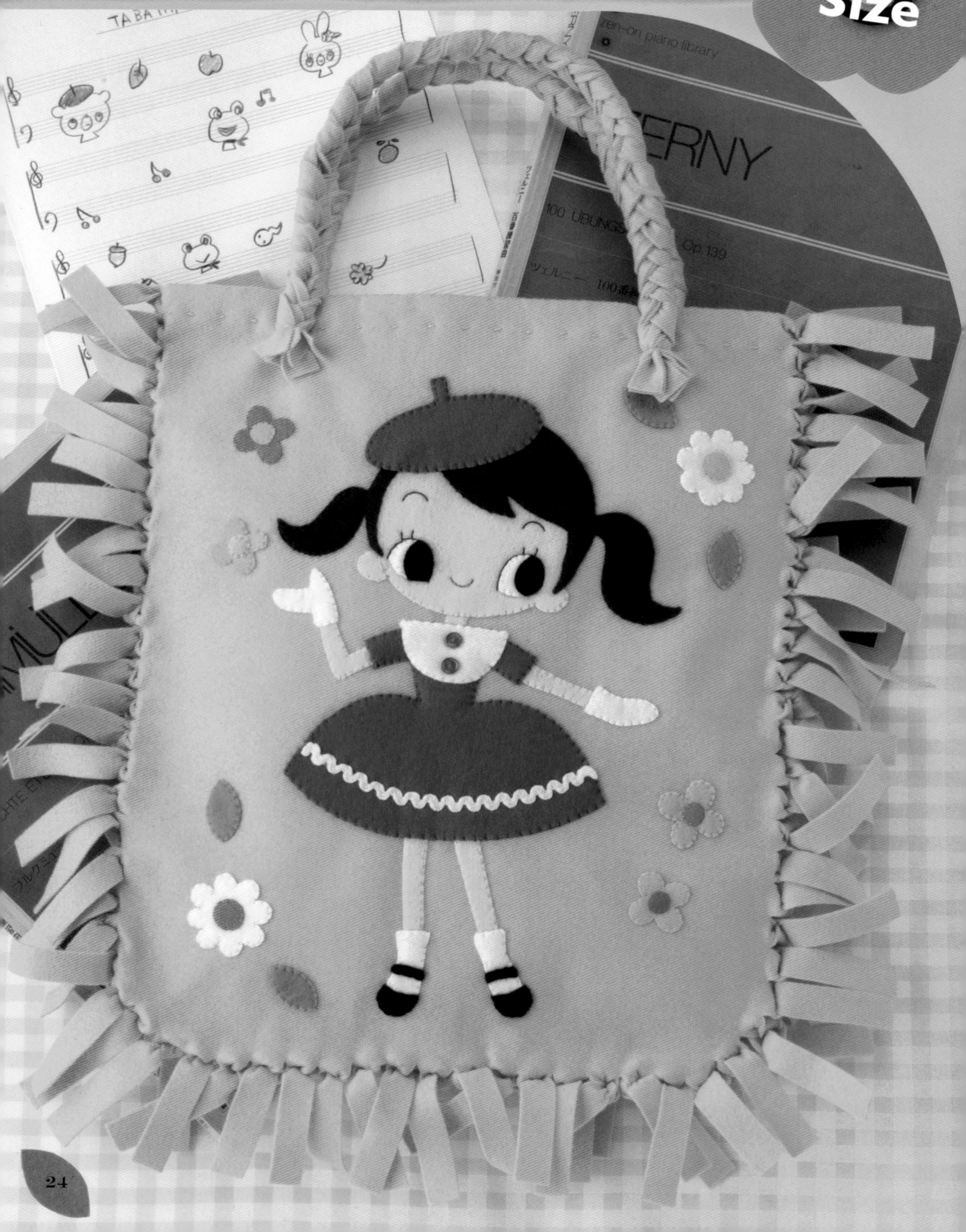

These adorable fringed bags are made by cutting and tying felt together— there's only a tiny bit of sewing involved. The braided handles are cute, too!

instructions P 52

Quick-tie Bags with Handles

These bags are just the right size for a notebook. They look great in deep red or marbled gray—and other colors too!

Medium Size

instructions P. 52

Quick-tie Bags with Handles

Made with 2 pieces of felt, these bags are so easy, once you start making them you won't want to stop.

Small Size

You can attach the appliqué with glue.

instructions P. 52

27

Sweet Cell Phone Pouch

These are the easiest to make in the "quick-tie" series. They don't require a needle or thread, and they bring back happy memories of childhood craft projects. You could make them to match the larger sized bags for a cute combination.

Handy Hints Before You Start

Basic Stitches

In this book, "stitch" means to use whipstitch, also called overstitch.

Match up the edges of two pieces of fabric and make one stitch at a time by "wrapping" the needle and thread around the edges.

The simple stitch below is used to attach appliqué.

Work one stitch at a time around the appliqué, making sure the stitches are perpendicular to the edge of the appliqué.

Embroidery Stitches

backstitch
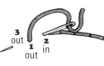

chain stitch
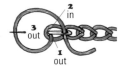

satin stitch
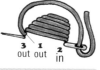

outline stitch
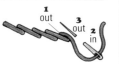

blanket stitch
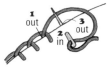

straight stitch

French knot stitch
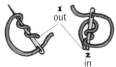

Attaching Eyes

Where there are no instructions, decide where you want to position the eyes, then glue on first the eyes and then the pupils.

You Will Need

Felt — Felt can basically be divided into two types: wool and washable. Wool felt is recommended for the projects in this book.

Needle	Scissors	Thread	Glue	Stuffing
Embroidery needle	Fabric scissors Paper scissors	Embroidery floss (size 25)	Woodworking glue	Polyester fiber stuffing

Embroidery Floss

Six fine strands make up one thread of embroidery floss. In this book, unless otherwise specified, "stitch" or "embroider" means you should use two strands of embroidery floss. Simply cut the floss to the length you need and separate two strands from it. Use the same color embroidery floss as the felt, and refer to the photographs for the colors needed for noses and mouths.

Using Patterns

To stop patterns from slipping on the felt, secure them with pins or stick double-sided tape to the back of the patterns. Make sure your fabric chalk is sharp. Follow instructions below for patterns marked "center line."

The dotted line marked "center line" is the center line of the shape you are cutting out. Cut the felt out in the following order:

1 Place pattern on one side of the felt, with the dotted line in the center (leaving room for the other half of the shape on the other side of the felt). Trace around the pattern outline with fabric chalk.

2 Keeping the center line in the center of the felt, move pattern to other side and trace the pattern outline as before.

3 Remove pattern and cut felt out along line marked in fabric chalk. Cut out center part of shape if necessary.

The instruction "sew on wrong side" on a pattern piece indicates that the piece needs to be sewn from the reverse side of the fabric so that stitches do not show from the front.

Stuffing

Stuff narrow points of parts such as legs and snouts first, inserting stuffing little by little until shape is firm.

Naomi's tip

When stuffing small objects I use a bamboo skewer with the end blunted.

Cute Felt Badges

Add a cool twist to appliqué with these felt badges. They're so simple—all you have to do is appliqué designs onto a felt base, and then cut around the outline.

instructions ⓟ 56~58

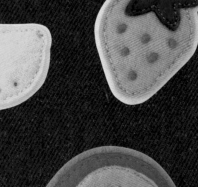

Pocket-sized Playmates
Best Buddies

Yellow Puppy Dog and Orange Puppy Dog

How to Make

large photo P.7

Back

1. Fold sides of underbody piece together and stitch the center closed on the wrong side.
2. Stitch dart on each body piece.
3. Open out underbody piece and stitch to both body pieces as shown in diagram. Stitch left and right body pieces together up to ▼ mark.
4. Stitch back closed, inserting stuffing as you go.
5. Sandwich body piece between two nose pieces and stitch together. Attach eyes and ears with glue.

Felt to Use

yellow: 5 1/2" x 3 1/2"
orange: 5 1/2" x 3 1/2"
dark green: 2" x 2"
purple: 2" x 2"
white: 2 3/4" x 2" (for each dog)
scraps of black and dark brown

body x 2
underbody x 1
ear x 2
○ eye x 2
● pupil x 2
● nose x 2

Start 1

wrong side

2

dart

3

start stitching from here

right side

4

stuffing

5

Finish

Pattern Actual Size

nose x 2

body x 2

eye x 2

pupil x 2

ear x 2

underbody x 1
sew on wrong side

dart

"sew on wrong side" means that stitches should not show on the right side of the fabric

See P.29 for information about patterns.

32

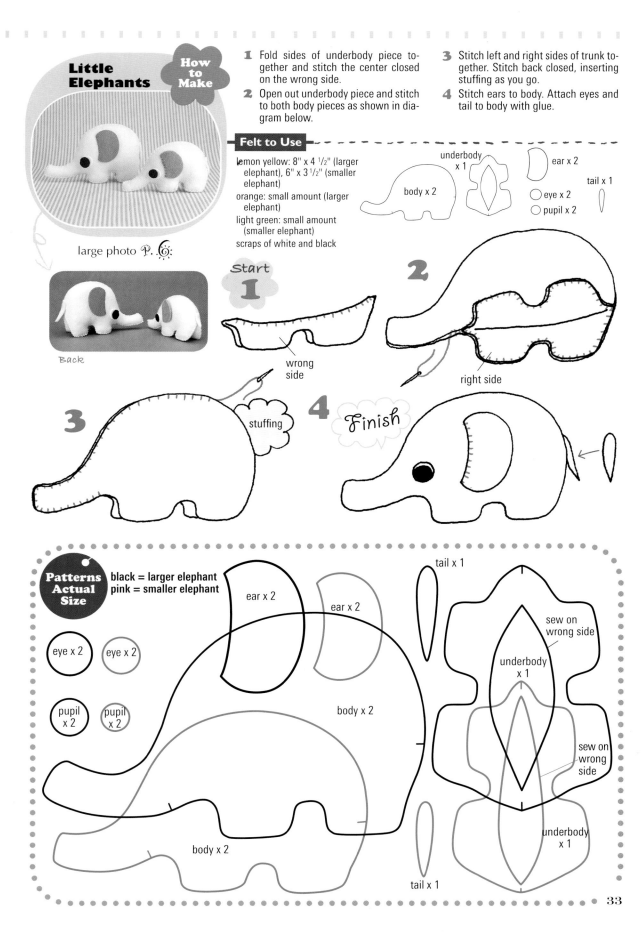

Little Elephants

How to Make

1. Fold sides of underbody piece together and stitch the center closed on the wrong side.
2. Open out underbody piece and stitch to both body pieces as shown in diagram below.
3. Stitch left and right sides of trunk together. Stitch back closed, inserting stuffing as you go.
4. Stitch ears to body. Attach eyes and tail to body with glue.

large photo P. 6

Back

Felt to Use

lemon yellow: 8" x 4 1/2" (larger elephant), 6" x 3 1/2" (smaller elephant)
orange: small amount (larger elephant)
light green: small amount (smaller elephant)
scraps of white and black

underbody x 1
body x 2
ear x 2
eye x 2
pupil x 2
tail x 1

Start
1
wrong side

2
right side

3
stuffing

4 Finish

Patterns Actual Size

black = larger elephant
pink = smaller elephant

ear x 2
ear x 2
eye x 2
eye x 2
pupil x 2
pupil x 2
body x 2
body x 2
tail x 1
tail x 1
sew on wrong side
underbody x 1
sew on wrong side
underbody x 1

Mom and Baby Kitty Cats

How to Make

large photo P. 6

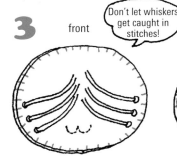

Back

1. Embroider mouth onto front of head and attach whiskers as shown in diagram.

2. Fold back of head in half and stitch base closed for about 1/4" as shown in diagram.

3. Join **1** and **2** together by stitching around edge. Insert stuffing through back of head.

4. Fold sides of underbody piece together and stitch the center closed on the wrong side.

5. Stitch underbody and body pieces together up to ▶ mark as shown in diagram. Stitch back closed, inserting stuffing as you go.

6. Insert neck into base of head and stitch to secure.

7. Stitch ears to head. Stitch tail sections together, insert stuffing, and stitch to body. Attach eyes with glue. Spread glue onto whiskers to stiffen them, and trim.

Felt to Use

black: 8" x 4 3/4" (Mom)
8" x 3 1/4" (Baby)
scraps of white and blue

head (front) x 1

head (back) x 1

body x 2

underbody x 1

● **Patterns on p. 58**

 ear x 2

 eye x 2

 pupil x 2

tail x 2

Start

1

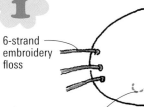

6-strand embroidery floss

backstitch

right side

wrong side

knot

2

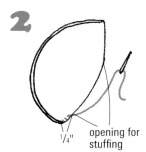

1/4"

opening for stuffing

3

front

Don't let whiskers get caught in stitches!

back

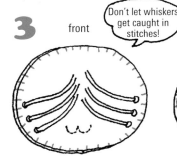

stuffing

4

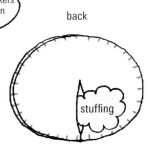

wrong side

5 ▶

stuffing

right side

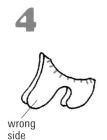

6

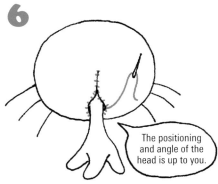

The positioning and angle of the head is up to you.

7

Finish

stuffing

Using fingers, spread glue along whiskers to stiffen, and trim to same length when dry.

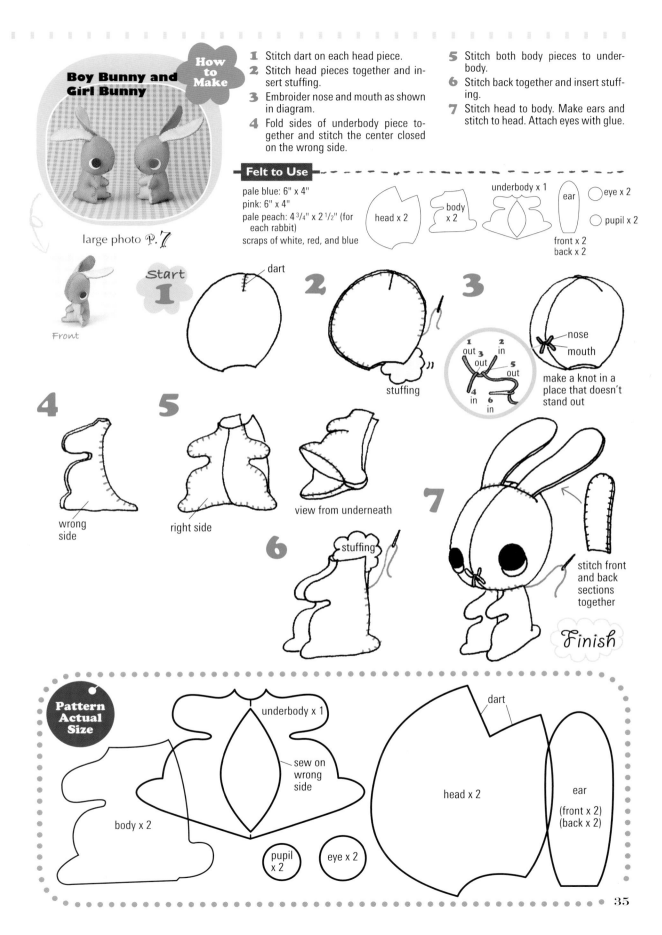

Boy Bunny and Girl Bunny

How to Make

1 Stitch dart on each head piece.
2 Stitch head pieces together and insert stuffing.
3 Embroider nose and mouth as shown in diagram.
4 Fold sides of underbody piece together and stitch the center closed on the wrong side.
5 Stitch both body pieces to underbody.
6 Stitch back together and insert stuffing.
7 Stitch head to body. Make ears and stitch to head. Attach eyes with glue.

large photo P.7

Front

Felt to Use

pale blue: 6" x 4"
pink: 6" x 4"
pale peach: 4 3/4" x 2 1/2" (for each rabbit)
scraps of white, red, and blue

head x 2   body x 2   underbody x 1   ear   eye x 2   pupil x 2   front x 2   back x 2

Start
1

dart

2   stuffing

3   nose   mouth
out 1 2 in
out 3
out 4 in 5 out
6 in
make a knot in a place that doesn't stand out

4   wrong side

5   right side   view from underneath

6   stuffing

7   stitch front and back sections together

Finish

Pattern Actual Size

body x 2

underbody x 1

sew on wrong side

pupil x 2   eye x 2

dart

head x 2

ear
(front x 2)
(back x 2)

35

Pocket-sized Playmates
One Pattern, Eight Playmates

Bearly There and Friends

How to Make

Choose the face (**3**) and finishing details (**5**) for the character you want to make.

1 Fold smaller "body" section of each body-and-head piece up against "head" section, and stitch to close gap. For Mini Hana Hood only, cut along line indicated in diagram. Use cut-off section as the pattern for her underpants, which should be a different color to the rest of the body-and-head piece. Sew underpants section back onto body-and-head piece.

2 Stitch darts on body-and-head piece.

3 Excluding eyes, attach all face parts to head, either by embroidery or appliqué.

4 Stitch body-and-head piece closed, inserting stuffing as you go.

5 Make ears, arms, legs, and other body parts and stitch to body. Attach eyes with glue.

photos P.8~9

Back

Felt to Use

The first color after the character's name is the main color and 8" x 6" is required.
Only a small amount is required for each of the other colors listed.

a Bearly There: red, pale peach, white, black

b Little Black Cat: black, pink, white, blue

c Croaky Frog: green, white, black

d Cuddly Koala: light blue, dark brown, white, black

e Panda Pal: white, black

f Droopy-eared Dog: lemon yellow, brown, white, black

g Cheeky Monkey: pink, pale peach, white, black

h Mini Hana Hood: pale peach, red (each 6" x 6"), blue, white, black

Pattern on p. 59

Start 1

body-and-head piece

right side

Mini Hana Hood

neck section   wrong side

cutting line

2

dart (5 places)

3

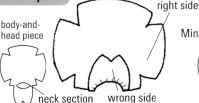

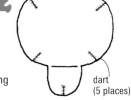

a Bearly There

straight stitch (applies to all below)

3/8"

3/8"

satin stitch (applies to all below)

b Little Black Cat

knot

3/8"

3/8"

1/4"

backstitch (applies to all below)

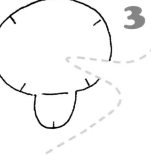

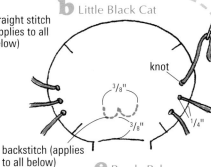

c Croaky Frog

1 1/4"

5/8"

d Cuddly Koala

3/8"

3/8"

stuffing

e Panda Pal

3/8"

3/8"

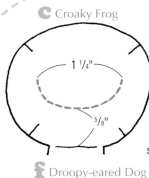
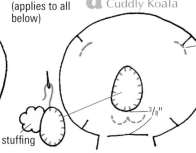
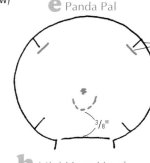

f Droopy-eared Dog

5/8"

stuffing

3/8"

g Cheeky Monkey

1/16"

h Mini Hana Hood

5/8"

1"

3/8"

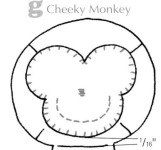

36

* Illustrations are not to scale.

4

stuffing

5 Finish

You can also use 6-strand embroidery floss for the neck ribbon.

b Little Black Cat

a Bearly There

stuffing

thin strip of felt (6 1/4" x 1/8")

rear view

c Croaky Frog

1"

stuffing

e Panda Pal

cut out the center of the circle to form a ring

d Cuddly Koala

fold in half

rear view

f Droopy-eared Dog

Attach with glue.

stuffing

rear view

g Cheeky Monkey

rear view

h Mini Hana Hood

attach bangs

wind 6-strand embroidery floss around thick card 8 times

1"

Attach with glue.

tie together

side view

make hood and put on head

6-strand embroidery floss

fold down point of hood and stitch to secure

attach arms to dress

Glue on.

Brown Bear's Buddies

Trouser Bear

How to Make

large photo P.12

Back   *Side*

Trouser Bear is assembled in basically the same way as Brown Bear (see p. 11).

1. Stitch upper face to lower face. The rest of the head is made in the same way as for Brown Bear, except for the embroidered mouth.

2. Stitch upper body to lower body. Stitch base to lower body. Assembly is the same as for Brown Bear, except for the positioning of the legs. Stitch legs, arms, and tail to body in that order.

3. Attach eyes, nose, suspenders, and buttons with glue.

Felt to Use

light blue: 8" x 8"
orange: 6" x 6"
ivory: 6" x 4"
scraps of yellow, dark brown, white, and black

Pattern on p. 60

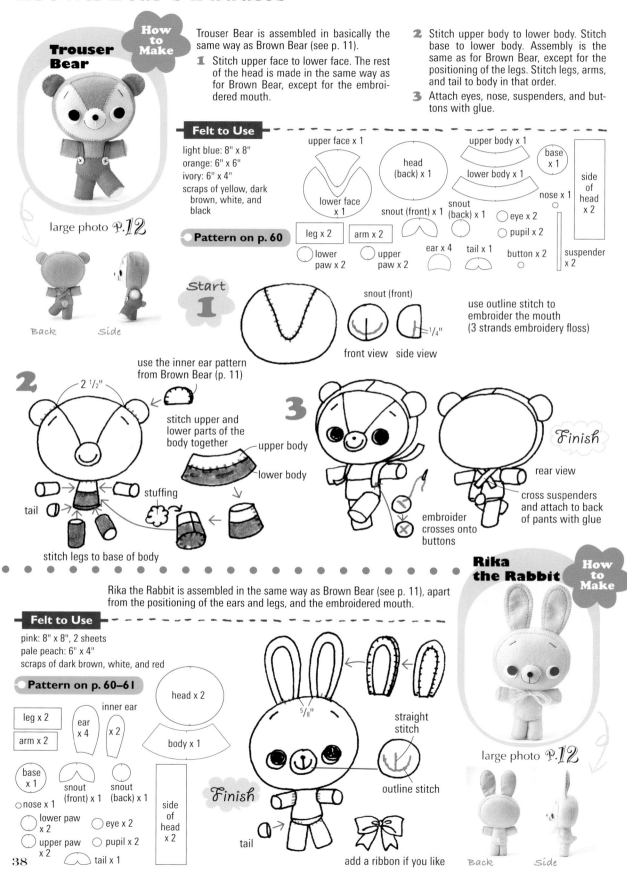

upper face x 1
lower face x 1
head (back) x 1
upper body x 1
lower body x 1
base x 1
side of head x 2
snout (front) x 1
snout (back) x 1
nose x 1
eye x 2
pupil x 2
leg x 2
arm x 2
ear x 4
tail x 1
button x 2
suspender x 2
lower paw x 2
upper paw x 2

Start 1

snout (front)

front view   side view

¼"

use outline stitch to embroider the mouth (3 strands embroidery floss)

2

2 ½"

use the inner ear pattern from Brown Bear (p. 11)

stitch upper and lower parts of the body together

upper body
lower body

tail
stuffing

stitch legs to base of body

3

embroider crosses onto buttons

Finish

rear view

cross suspenders and attach to back of pants with glue

Rika the Rabbit

How to Make

Rika the Rabbit is assembled in the same way as Brown Bear (see p. 11), apart from the positioning of the ears and legs, and the embroidered mouth.

Felt to Use

pink: 8" x 8", 2 sheets
pale peach: 6" x 4"
scraps of dark brown, white, and red

Pattern on p. 60–61

leg x 2
arm x 2
inner ear
ear x 4
inner ear x 2
head x 2
body x 1
base x 1
snout (front) x 1
snout (back) x 1
nose x 1
lower paw x 2
upper paw x 2
eye x 2
pupil x 2
tail x 1
side of head x 2

⅝"

straight stitch

outline stitch

Finish

tail

add a ribbon if you like

large photo P.12

Back   *Side*

Hana Hood

How to Make

Hana Hood is assembled in basically the same way as Brown Bear (see p. 11).

1. Embroider eyebrows, eyelashes, and mouth to front of head. Stitch sides of head to both head pieces and insert stuffing from back of head.
2. Create bangs with embroidery floss, and glue into position as shown in diagram.
3. Stitch legs and shoes together, make legs, and stitch to body.
4. Stitch dress together at back and position on body with a few stitches.
5. Stitch head to body. Make arms and stitch to body over dress.
6. Stitch darts in hood. Fold in half and stitch down center, leaving about 1 1/4" open at base.
7. Stitch hood to head.
8. Glue eyes to face and ribbon under chin.

large photo P.13

Back   *Side*

*For the benefit of beginners, the eyelashes have been made in a simpler way from those shown on p. 13.

Felt to Use

pale peach: 8" x 8", 2 sheets
white: 4 3/4" x 4"
red: 12" x 4"
dark green: 5 1/8" x 2 1/2"
scraps of earth tone and black

Pattern on p. 60–61

head x 2 · body x 1 · base x 1 · side of head x 2 · center line · hood x 1 · arm x 2 · dress x 1 · leg x 2 · sole of shoe x 2 · shoe x 2 · hood ribbon x 1 · eye x 2 · pupil x 2

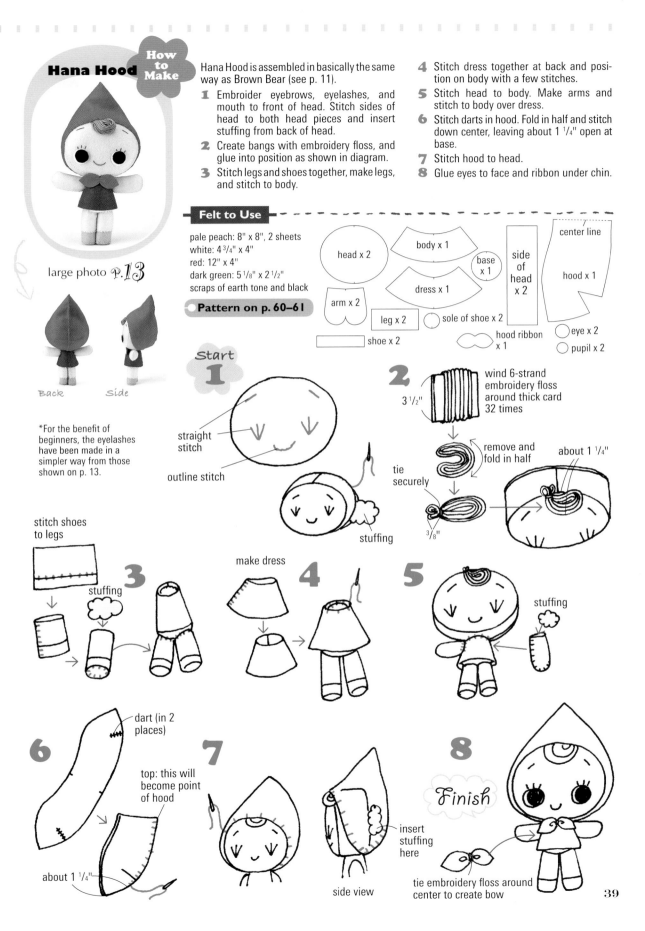

Start 1

straight stitch
outline stitch
stuffing

2
3 1/2"
wind 6-strand embroidery floss around thick card 32 times
remove and fold in half
tie securely
3/8"
about 1 1/4"

3
stitch shoes to legs
stuffing

4
make dress

5
stuffing

6
dart (in 2 places)
top: this will become point of hood
about 1 1/4"

7
side view
insert stuffing here

8
Finish
tie embroidery floss around center to create bow

39

Tabletop Duo

Kenji the Cat

How to Make

large photo P. *14*

Back   Side

1. Fold sides of underbody piece together and stitch the center closed on the wrong side.
2. Stitch both body pieces to underbody.
3. Leaving a gap to insert stuffing, stitch neck section of body. Stitch the back together from bottom upwards, inserting stuffing as you go.
4. Stitch darts on both head pieces.
5. Embroider nose and mouth to front of head, and attach whiskers as shown in diagram (leave longer than desired to allow for trimming later).
6. Stitch front and back of head together, inserting stuffing as you go.
7. Insert neck section of the body into head and stitch in place.
8. Make ears and tail and stitch to head and body. Attach eyes with glue. Spread glue onto whiskers to stiffen them, and trim.

Felt to Use

black: 8" x 8", 3 sheets
scraps of gray, white, and blue

Pattern on p. 62

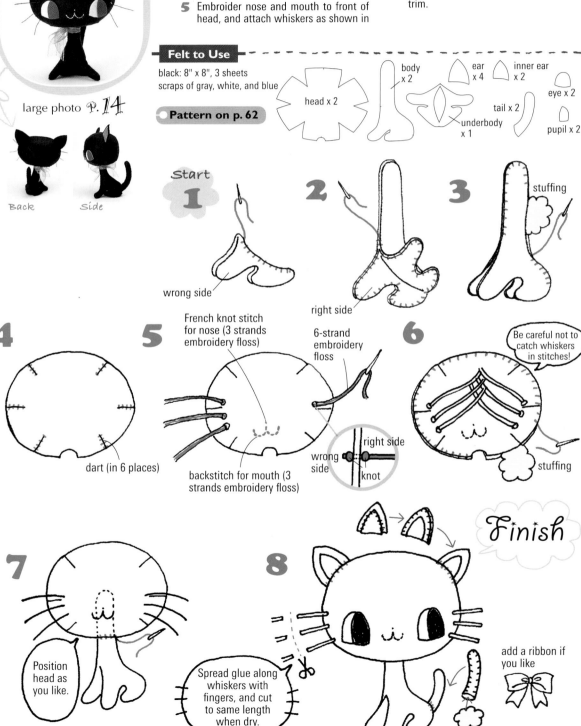

40

Mr. Sausage Dog

How to Make

1. Fold legs back against underbody piece. Stitch gaps closed at leg joints on the wrong side. Fold sides of underbody piece together and stitch the center closed on the wrong side.
2. Stitch both body pieces to underbody.
3. Stitch both sides of body together, inserting stuffing as you go.
4. Stitch neck to body and insert stuffing.
5. Stitch one face piece to side of head.
6. Stitch other face piece to other side of head and stitch underside of face sections closed.
7. Stitch back of head closed, inserting stuffing as you go.
8. Insert neck into head and stitch securely to body.
9. Embroider mouth and eyebrows. Stitch nose to end of snout and attach eyes with glue. Make ears and tail and stitch to head and body.

large photo P.15

Back   Front

Felt to Use

brown: 16" x 16", 2 sheets
pale peach: 5 1/2" x 4 3/4"
scraps of white and black

face x 2

body x 2

underbody x 1

sides of head x 1

ear

neck x 1

tail x 2

front x 2
back x 2

eye x 2

pupil x 2

nose x 1

Pattern on reverse of dust jacket

Start **1**

wrong side

right side

leg joint (in 4 places)

right side

2

3   stuffing

4   stuffing

5

6

7   stuffing

8   Position head as you like.

9   mouth

stuffing
wrong side
stitch loosely around edge and pull to tighten
right side

1 out   3 out   2 in   4 in

3 strands embroidery floss

straight stitch (3 strands embroidery floss)

Finish

stuffing

41

Forest Friends

Fumiko Fawn

How to Make

large photo P.16

Back   Front

large photo P.16

1. Stitch darts on center-of-head piece. Stitch dart on each face piece.
2. Stitch one face piece to side of head.
3. Stitch other face piece to other side of head and stitch underside of face sections closed.
4. Stitch back of head closed, inserting stuffing as you go.
5. Make ears and nose and stitch them to head. Embroider mouth. Glue first eyes and then pupils onto face.
6. Fold sides of underbody piece together and stitch the center closed on the wrong side. Fold legs back against underbody piece and stitch the gaps closed at leg joints on the wrong side.
7. Stitch body pieces to underbody.
8. Stitch back closed, inserting stuffing as you go.
9. Make tail and stitch to body. Glue markings to body.
10. Insert neck into head and stitch securely.

Felt to Use

pink: 8" x 8", 2 sheets
ivory: 8" x 8", 2 sheets
scraps of dark brown, white, and black

face x 2
ear
front x 2
back x 2
body x 2
underbody x 1
tail x 2
center of head x 1
eye x 2
pupil x 2
nose
markings x 6

Pattern on reverse of dust jacket

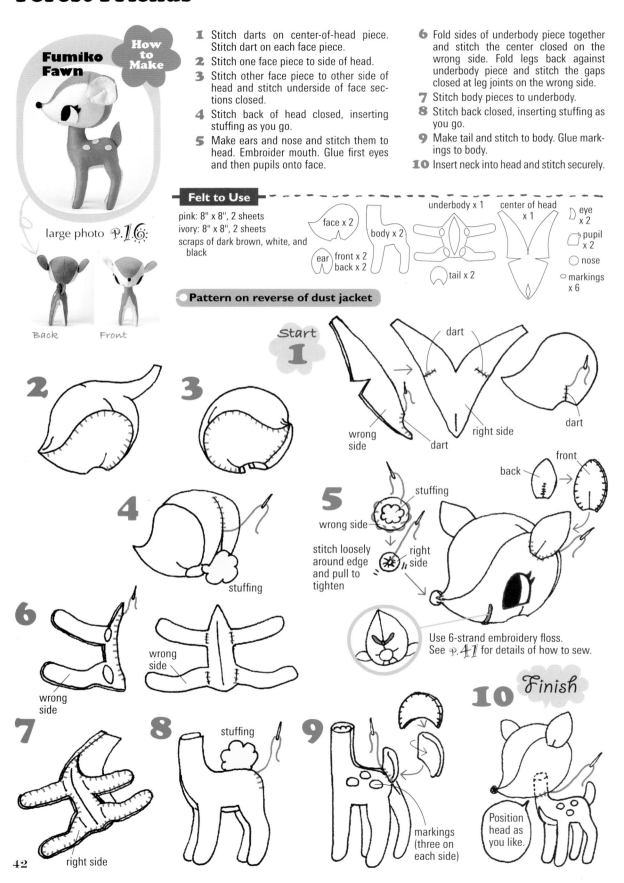

Start 1

dart
wrong side
dart
right side
dart

back   front

2

3

4
stuffing

5
stuffing
wrong side
stitch loosely around edge and pull to tighten
right side

Use 6-strand embroidery floss. See P.41 for details of how to sew.

See P.41 for details of how to sew.

6
wrong side
wrong side

7
right side

8
stuffing

9
markings (three on each side)

10 Finish
Position head as you like.

42

Little Rabbit

large photo P.17

 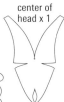

How to Make

To make Little Rabbit's head (apart from the ears), follow steps **1–5** for Fumiko Fawn (see facing page).

1 Make ears and stitch to head.
2 Stitch the gaps closed at arm and leg joints on the wrong side.
3 Stitch body pieces to underbody.
4 Stitch ³/₄" up center of back, starting at bottom.
5 Stitch base to body.
6 Stitch center of back together, inserting stuffing as you go.
7 Make tail and stitch to body.
8 Insert neck into head and stitch securely.

Felt to Use

blue: 8" x 8", 1 ¹/₂ sheets
pale peach: 8" x 8"
pale pink: 3 ¹/₄" x 2 ¹/₂"
scraps of dark brown, white, and black

face x 2
center of head x 1
base x 1
ear x 4
inner ear x 2
body x 2
underbody x 1
tail x 2
eye x 2
nose x 1
pupil x 2

Back   Front

● **Pattern on reverse of dust jacket**

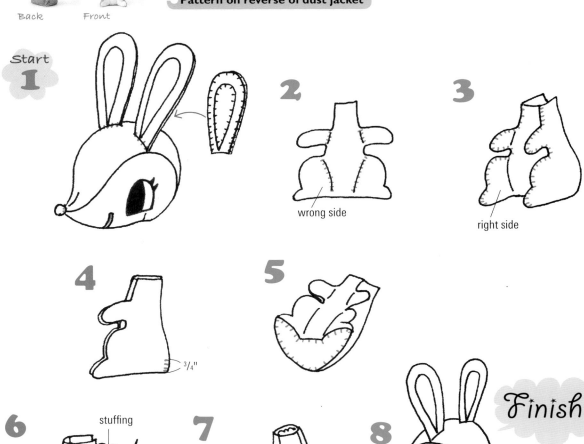

Start **1**

2 wrong side

3 right side

4 ³/₄"

5

6 stuffing

7

8

Finish

Beret Buddies

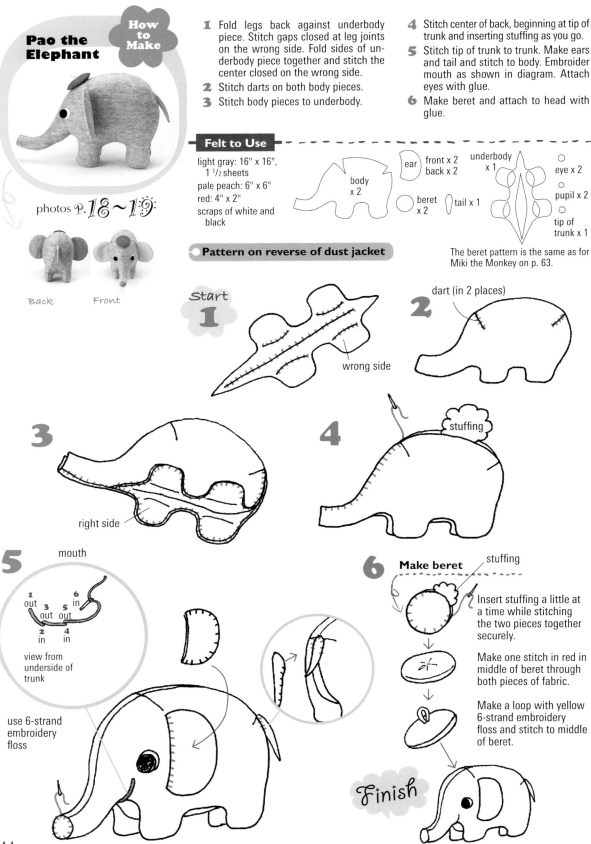

Pao the Elephant

How to Make

photos P.18~19

Back   Front

1. Fold legs back against underbody piece. Stitch gaps closed at leg joints on the wrong side. Fold sides of underbody piece together and stitch the center closed on the wrong side.
2. Stitch darts on both body pieces.
3. Stitch body pieces to underbody.
4. Stitch center of back, beginning at tip of trunk and inserting stuffing as you go.
5. Stitch tip of trunk to trunk. Make ears and tail and stitch to body. Embroider mouth as shown in diagram. Attach eyes with glue.
6. Make beret and attach to head with glue.

Felt to Use

light gray: 16" x 16", 1 1/2 sheets
pale peach: 6" x 6"
red: 4" x 2"
scraps of white and black

body x 2   ear   front x 2 / back x 2   underbody x 1   eye x 2
beret x 2   tail x 1   pupil x 2
tip of trunk x 1

The beret pattern is the same as for Miki the Monkey on p. 63.

Pattern on reverse of dust jacket

Start 1
wrong side

2 dart (in 2 places)

3 right side

4 stuffing

5 mouth
1 out 6 in
3 out 5 out
2 in 4 in
view from underside of trunk

use 6-strand embroidery floss

6 Make beret   stuffing

Insert stuffing a little at a time while stitching the two pieces together securely.

Make one stitch in red in middle of beret through both pieces of fabric.

Make a loop with yellow 6-strand embroidery floss and stitch to middle of beret.

Finish

Miki the Monkey

How to Make

1. Appliqué face to front of head.
2. Make snout and stitch to front of head.
3. Embroider mouth on snout.
4. Stitch bottom edges of side of head together to form a ring, then stitch front and back pieces of head to ring. Insert stuffing as you stitch on back of head.
5. Make ears and stitch to head.
6. Stitch body pieces together, insert stuffing, and stitch head to body.
7. Make arms, legs, and tail and stitch to body.
8. Make beret (see facing page) and glue to head. Attach eyes and nose with glue.

Felt to Use

yellow: 8" x 8"
pale peach: 5" x 3 1/2"
red: 4" x 2"
scraps of dark brown, white, and black

photos P.18~19

Back   Side

Pattern on p. 63

head x 2
body x 3
side of head x 1
face x 1
leg x 2
ear x 4
tail x 1
beret x 2
eye x 2
pupil x 2
nose x 1
arm x 2
hand x 4
lower paw x 4
inner ear x 2
snout x 1
back of snout x 1

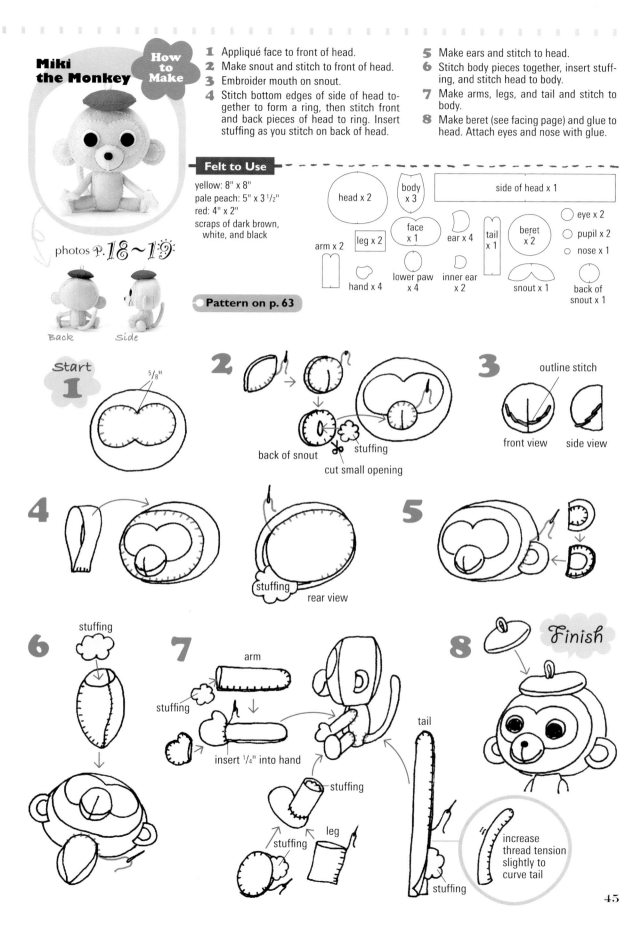

Start
1
5/8"

2
back of snout
cut small opening
stuffing

3
outline stitch
front view   side view

4
stuffing
rear view

5

6
stuffing

7
arm
stuffing
insert 1/4" into hand
stuffing
stuffing   leg
stuffing

tail
increase thread tension slightly to curve tail
stuffing

8   Finish
tail

Cute 'n' Fun Accessories

Coin Purses
Panda, Frog, Monkey, Elephant, and Chick

How to Make

photos 𝓟. 20~21

Basic assembly of all coin purses is the same as for the Panda Coin Purse below.

1 Stitch eyes and mouth onto face and embroider nose.

2 The zipper should measure the length indicated by the star, plus 1 1/4". Measure from the bottom end of zipper and cut, leaving an extra 1/4" at the top of zipper. Stitch several times over the topmost teeth of zipper to prevent it coming open.

3 Stitch front and back of coin purse to zipper so that 1/4" of zipper edge on each side lies under edges of purse.

4 Stitch lower edges of coin purse closed.

5 Avoiding zipper teeth, stitch ends of zipper to both sides of coin purse.

6 Make ears and stitch to back of coin purse.

Felt to Use

A sheet of felt measures 8" x 8". If felt size is not mentioned, only a small quantity is required.

Panda	Monkey	Elephant	Chick	Frog
white: 1 sheet	pink: 1 sheet	light gray: 2 sheets	yellow: 2 sheets	light green: 2 sheets
black: 5 1/8" x 4"	pale peach: 4 3/4" x 3 1/2"	orange: 5 1/8" x 4"	pink: 4 3/4" x 3 1/2"	white, black
pink	black, white	white, black	orange, red, white, blue	

You will also need

8" zipper (same color as coin purse)

Patterns on reverse of dust jacket

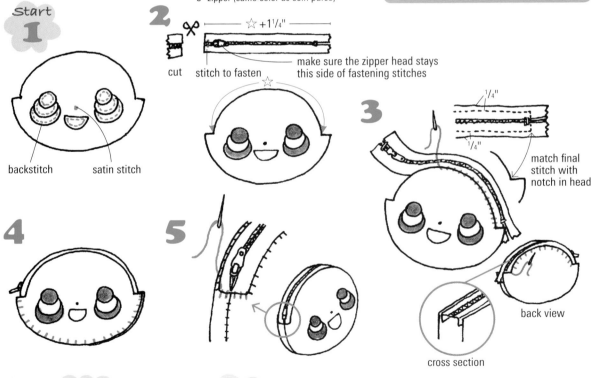

Start 1

backstitch   satin stitch

2   ☆ +1 1/4"

cut   stitch to fasten   make sure the zipper head stays this side of fastening stitches

3   1/4"   1/4"   match final stitch with notch in head

back view

4

5   cross section

6   *Finish*

back view

For the Frog Coin Purse and the Monkey Coin Purse

As for the Panda Coin Purse, stitch eyes and mouth to face before attaching zipper. For the Frog Coin Purse, the zipper is attached under the chin.

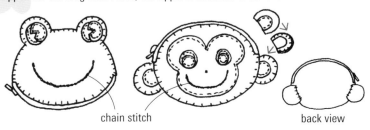

chain stitch   back view

For the Elephant Coin Purse and the Chick Coin Purse

Stitch eyes, ears, wings, and other parts to both sides of the body and follow instructions on facing page up to step **4**. For Elephant, fold sides of underbody piece together, stitch center on wrong side, and stitch underbody to body pieces. For Chick Coin Purse, insert legs and beak into body before stitching together.

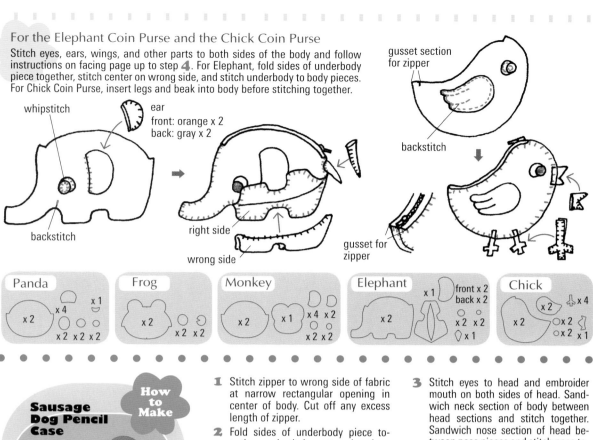

whipstitch

ear
front: orange x 2
back: gray x 2

backstitch

right side

wrong side

gusset section for zipper

backstitch

gusset for zipper

Panda	Frog	Monkey	Elephant	Chick

Panda: x 2, x 4, x 1, x 2 x 2 x 2

Frog: x 2, x 2 x 2

Monkey: x 2, x 1, x 4 x 2, x 2 x 2

Elephant: x 2, x 1, front x 2 back x 2, x 2 x 2, x 1

Chick: x 2, x 2, x 4, x 2, x 2 x 1

Sausage Dog Pencil Case

How to Make

large photo P.20

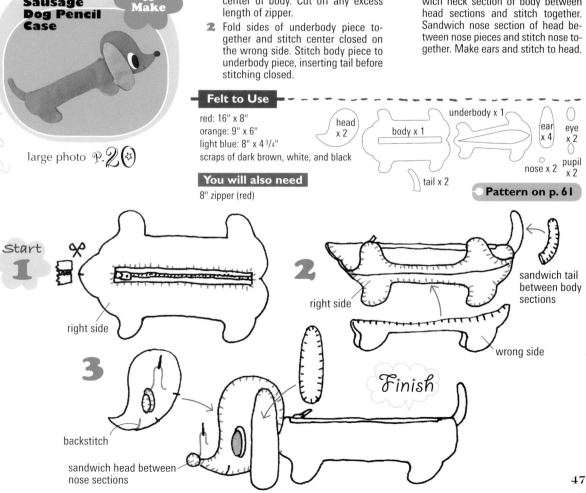

1 Stitch zipper to wrong side of fabric at narrow rectangular opening in center of body. Cut off any excess length of zipper.

2 Fold sides of underbody piece together and stitch center closed on the wrong side. Stitch body piece to underbody piece, inserting tail before stitching closed.

3 Stitch eyes to head and embroider mouth on both sides of head. Sandwich neck section of body between head sections and stitch together. Sandwich nose section of head between nose pieces and stitch nose together. Make ears and stitch to head.

Felt to Use

red: 16" x 8"
orange: 9" x 6"
light blue: 8" x 4 3/4"
scraps of dark brown, white, and black

You will also need

8" zipper (red)

head x 2

body x 1

underbody x 1

ear x 4

eye x 2

nose x 2

pupil x 2

tail x 2

Pattern on p. 61

Start **1**

right side

2

right side

wrong side

sandwich tail between body sections

3

backstitch

Finish

sandwich head between nose sections

47

Semicircle Coin Purses

Little Bird, Frog, Black Cat, and Goldfish

photos *P.21*

How to Make

1. Stitch socket of snap fastener to fabric at point indicated on diagram below.
2. Appliqué or embroider eyes, mouth, etc., to flap section. Place flap section on reverse of **1**, sandwiching in ears, tails, etc., as shown in diagram for each coin purse before stitching flap to main section.
3. Blanket stitch along the straight edge of the pocket section (this will become the opening of the coin purse), then stitch stud of snap fastener to pocket. With snap fasteners facing out for both sections, stitch pocket section to main section.

Felt to Use

A sheet of felt measures 8" x 8". If felt size is not mentioned, only a small quantity is required.

Little Bird	Frog	Black Cat	Goldfish
blue: 1 sheet	green: 1 sheet	black: 1 sheet	orange: 1 sheet
yellow: 4 3/4" x 4"	white, black	gray, white, blue	white, black
scraps of red, white, and black			

You will also need

1 pair of 1/2" diameter snap fasteners for each coin purse

Patterns on p. 62–63

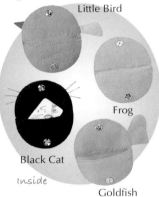

Little Bird

Frog

Black Cat

Goldfish

Inside

Start

1

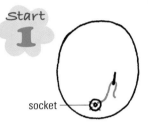

socket

Illustration shows frog version.

2

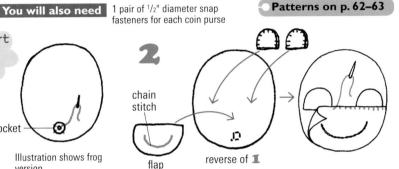

chain stitch

flap

reverse of **1**

Frog

For the frog only, appliqué the eyes and pupils last.

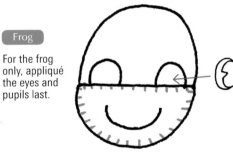

Little Bird

backstitch (applies to all below)

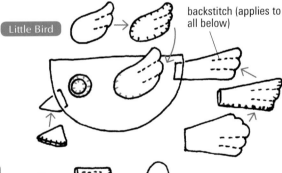

Black Cat

See *P.34* for how to make whiskers.

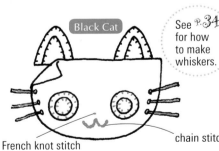

French knot stitch

chain stitch

Goldfish

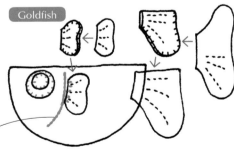

Finish

3

blanket stitch

stud

pocket

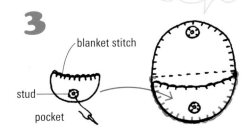

	All versions	Frog	Little Bird
main section	x 1	x 4 x 2 x 2	○ x 2 ○ x 2
flap	x 1		x 1 x 1
pocket	x 1	Black Cat	Goldfish
		x 4 x 2 ○ x 2	○ x 2 x 2

48

Little Bear Card Case and Card Case with Hearts

How to Make

1. Stitch snap fastener to front and back of main section of case as shown in diagram.
2. Blanket stitch along the fabric edge above the socket of the snap fastener.
3. Fold so that corners match up to ◎ marks. Blanket stitch the sides together.
4. For Little Bear's face, embroider eyes, nose, and mouth.
5. Position the appliqué pieces to conceal stitches for snap fastener or other stray threads.

photos P.21

Felt to Use

Little Bear Card Case
cream: 5 3/4" x 4"
scraps of red

Card Case with Hearts
black: 5 3/4" x 4"
scraps of pink

You will also need 1 pair 1/2" diameter snap fasteners for each case

main section x 1

Little Bear x 1
Heart x 3

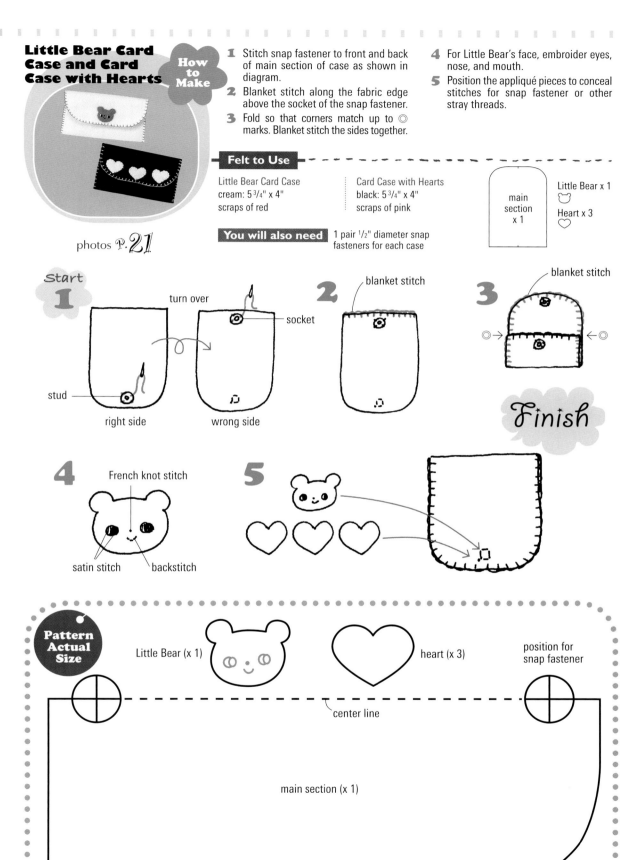

Start **1**

turn over

socket

stud

right side

wrong side

2 blanket stitch

3 blanket stitch

◎→ ←◎

Finish

4 French knot stitch

satin stitch   backstitch

5

Pattern Actual Size

Little Bear (x 1)   heart (x 3)   position for snap fastener

center line

main section (x 1)

Felt Flowers

------- 12 Items

photos P. 22~23

How to Make

These cute flowers are made simply by cutting and layering shapes, and securing them with beads, buttons, and other decorations. For flowers that are made of several layers, follow the numbers on the patterns and layer each piece in ascending numerical order.

Felt to Use

Refer to the colors used on p. 22–23. Use pattern pieces as a guide to calculate amount needed.

Patterns Actual Size

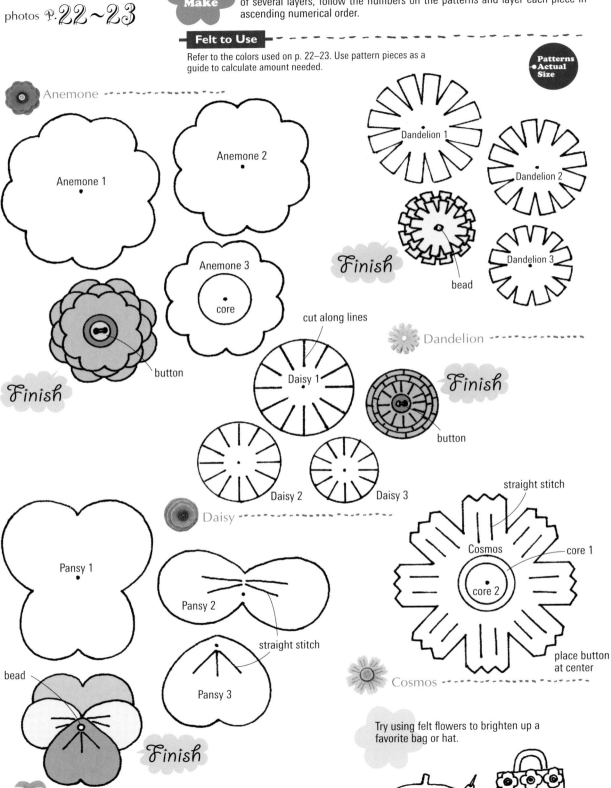

Anemone

Anemone 1

Anemone 2

Anemone 3

core

button

Finish

Dandelion 1

Dandelion 2

Dandelion 3

bead

Finish

Dandelion

cut along lines

Daisy 1

Daisy 2

Daisy 3

button

Daisy

Pansy 1

Pansy 2

Pansy 3

straight stitch

bead

Finish

Pansy

straight stitch

Cosmos

core 1

core 2

place button at center

Cosmos

Try using felt flowers to brighten up a favorite bag or hat.

50

Poppy

place button at center

Poppy

core 1
core 2

Marguerite

place button at center

Marguerite

Gerbera

Gerbera

core

place button at center

Rose

Finish

bead

Leopard Plant

Leopard Plant

place button at center

Rose 1

Rose 2

leaves

Rose 3

Rose 4

Rose 5

Hydrangea

place bead at center

Hydrangea

Pink

Try making a bouquet using artificial flower stems for a lifelike touch. If you're having trouble pushing the wire through the felt, make a hole with a large needle first.

Pink

Have a go with lots of different kinds of flowers!

bead

Finish

twist

Finish

button

secure tightly by twisting wire

rear view

Quick-tie Bags with Handles

How to Make

1. For all bag sizes, cut main section and handles following measurements in diagrams below.
2. Divide 12 strips for handles into 2 groups of 6. Divide each group into 3 sections of 2 strips each to braid. (Once complete there will be 2 handles.)
3. On both bag pieces, fold over the ³/₄" excess fabric at the opening of the bag to the wrong side and stitch using running stitch.
4. Stitch handles to bag.
5. Appliqué front of bag.
6. Cut fringing on both sides of bag and tie fringes together using square knots.

large photos P.24~27

→ See P.55 for appliqué patterns.

Start 1

Felt to Use

Apart from the main pieces, you will also need various colors to make flowers, fruit, etc.

Large Size: 48" x 24" of main color
8" x 6" of main color of appliquéd girl's outfit
scraps of other colors

Medium Size: 44" x 24" of main color
8" x 8" of appliquéd animal color
scraps of other colors

Small Size: 2 pieces of 16" x 16" of main color
8" x 8" of main appliqué color
scraps of other colors

When purchasing fabric off the roll, be sure to calculate the amount required and have the storekeeper cut a little more than necessary.

Diagram for Large Size   24" x 24" will yield one side and one handle.

To start, draft the measurements of the main part of the bag (the part between the fringing) onto the felt. Add ³/₄" at top for opening, 4" on left, right, and bottom for fringing, and cut felt.

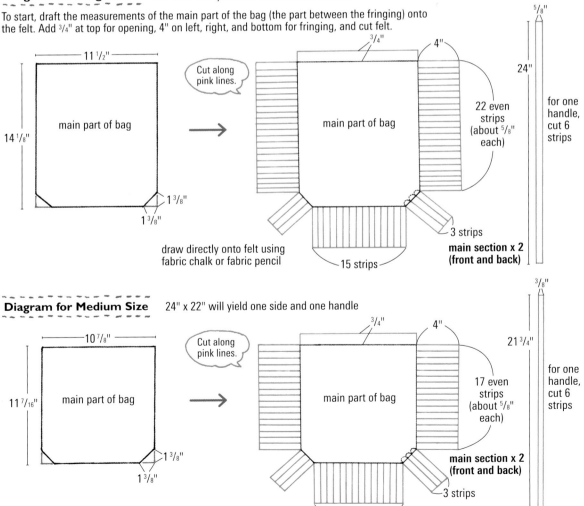

11 ¹/₂"

14 ¹/₈"

main part of bag

1 ³/₈"   1 ³/₈"

draw directly onto felt using fabric chalk or fabric pencil

Cut along pink lines.

³/₄"   4"

main part of bag

22 even strips (about ⁵/₈" each)

15 strips

3 strips

main section x 2 (front and back)

24"

⁵/₈"

for one handle, cut 6 strips

Diagram for Medium Size   24" x 22" will yield one side and one handle

10 ⁷/₈"

11 ⁷/₁₆"

main part of bag

1 ³/₈"   1 ³/₈"

Cut along pink lines.

³/₄"   4"

main part of bag

17 even strips (about ⁵/₈" each)

14 strips

3 strips

main section x 2 (front and back)

21 ³/₄"

³/₈"

for one handle, cut 6 strips

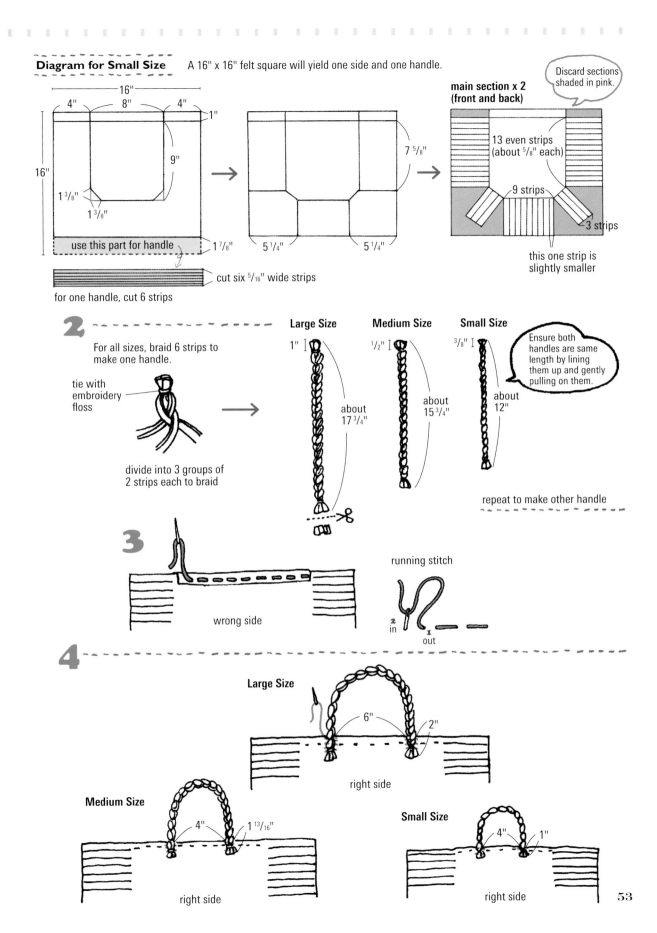

Diagram for Small Size — A 16" x 16" felt square will yield one side and one handle.

16"

4" 8" 4"

1"

9"

16"

$1^3/8$"

$1^3/8$"

use this part for handle

$1^7/8$"

cut six $5/16$" wide strips

for one handle, cut 6 strips

$7^5/8$"

$5^1/4$" $5^1/4$"

main section x 2 (front and back)

Discard sections shaded in pink.

13 even strips (about $5/8$" each)

9 strips

3 strips

this one strip is slightly smaller

2

For all sizes, braid 6 strips to make one handle.

tie with embroidery floss

divide into 3 groups of 2 strips each to braid

Large Size

1"

about $17^3/4$"

Medium Size

$1/2$"

about $15^3/4$"

Small Size

$3/8$"

about 12"

Ensure both handles are same length by lining them up and gently pulling on them.

repeat to make other handle

3

wrong side

running stitch

2 in

1 out

4

Large Size

6"

2"

right side

Medium Size

4"

$1^{13}/16$"

right side

Small Size

4"

1"

right side

53

5

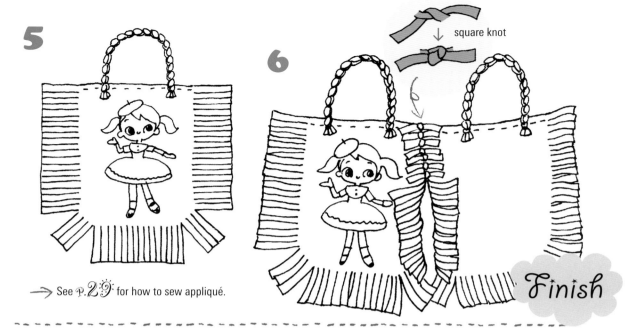

square knot

Finish

→ See P.29 for how to sew appliqué.

6

Sweet Cell Phone Pouch

How to Make

1 Cut felt as shown in diagram. To remove sections from inside handles, first make a small cut, then follow outline to cut and remove felt. Cut fringing on both sides of pouch.

2 Fold in half so handles match and join front and back sections together by knotting the fringing (see above). Attach appliqué with glue.

Felt to Use

16" x 8" of main color
scraps of color for appliqué

Diagram for Cell Phone Pouch

Discard sections shaded in pink.

large photo P.28

Start **1**

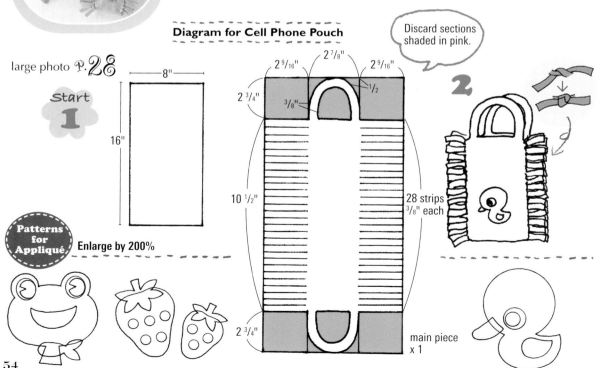

8"

16"

2 9/16"   2 7/8"   2 9/16"

2 3/4"   3/8"   1/2

10 1/2"

28 strips
3/8" each

2 3/4"

main piece
x 1

Patterns for Appliqué Enlarge by 200%

2

54

Patterns for Appliqué

Enlarge by 250%
You will also need rickrack and some very small buttons.

backstitch
chain stitch
French knot stitch
straight stitch

See P.29 for details of stitches.

center line

center line

Appliqué can be attached with glue.

Cute Felt Badges

 ---*25*Items

photos
P. *30~31*

How to Make

Attach felt appliqué to slightly larger felt base, then trim, leaving a narrow edge. Repeat this process for the heart and octopus badges, so that there are two layers of base felt.

Felt to Use

See photos on p. 30–31 for colors. Use pattern pieces as a guide to calculate amount needed.

Patterns ●Actual Size

- – – – – backstitch   • • • • French knot stitch
- chain stitch   outline stitch
- satin stitch | | | | | | whipstitch

See P. *29* for details.

LOVE

cocoa

For the rainbow stripes,
appliqué pink last.

SARUKUN

HAPPY

NAKAYOSHI

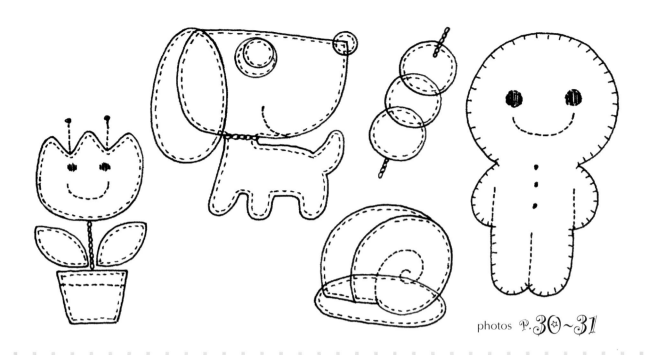

photos P.30~31

Mom and Baby Kitty Cats

photo p. 6

How to Make P.34

black pattern = Mom
pink pattern = Baby

For information about patterns, see P.29

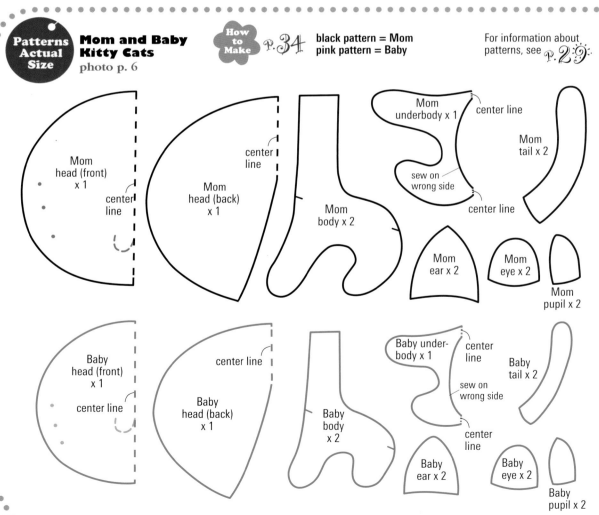

Mom head (front) x 1

center line

Mom head (back) x 1

center line

Mom body x 2

Mom underbody x 1

center line

sew on wrong side

center line

Mom tail x 2

Mom ear x 2

Mom eye x 2

Mom pupil x 2

Baby head (front) x 1

center line

center line

Baby head (back) x 1

Baby body x 2

Baby underbody x 1

center line

sew on wrong side

center line

Baby tail x 2

Baby ear x 2

Baby eye x 2

Baby pupil x 2

Pocket-sized Playmates
One Pattern, Eight Playmates
photos p. 8–9

How to Make P. 36

a Bearly There b Little Black Cat c Croaky Frog d Cuddly Koala e Panda Pal
f Droopy-eared Dog g Cheeky Monkey h Mini Hana Hood

Patterns Actual Size

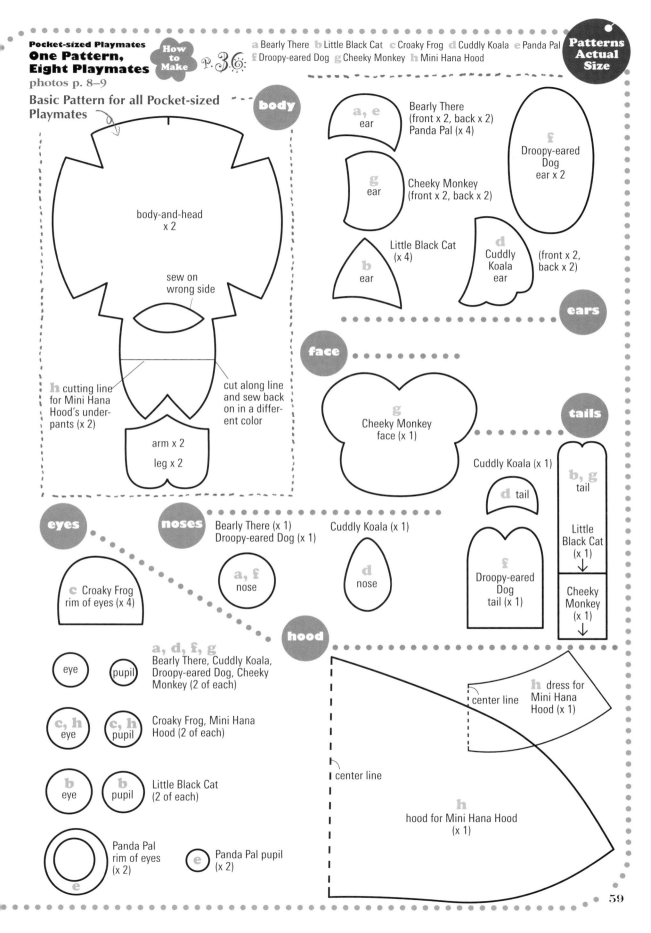

Basic Pattern for all Pocket-sized Playmates

body

body-and-head x 2

sew on wrong side

h cutting line for Mini Hana Hood's underpants (x 2)

cut along line and sew back on in a different color

arm x 2
leg x 2

ears

a, e ear Bearly There (front x 2, back x 2) Panda Pal (x 4)

g ear Cheeky Monkey (front x 2, back x 2)

b ear Little Black Cat (x 4)

d Cuddly Koala ear (front x 2, back x 2)

f Droopy-eared Dog ear x 2

face

g Cheeky Monkey face (x 1)

tails

Cuddly Koala (x 1)
d tail

f Droopy-eared Dog tail (x 1)

b, g tail
Little Black Cat (x 1)
↓
Cheeky Monkey (x 1)
↓

eyes

c Croaky Frog rim of eyes (x 4)

noses

Bearly There (x 1)
Droopy-eared Dog (x 1)
a, f nose

Cuddly Koala (x 1)
d nose

eye   pupil   a, d, f, g Bearly There, Cuddly Koala, Droopy-eared Dog, Cheeky Monkey (2 of each)

c, h eye   c, h pupil   Croaky Frog, Mini Hana Hood (2 of each)

b eye   b pupil   Little Black Cat (2 of each)

e Panda Pal rim of eyes (x 2)   e Panda Pal pupil (x 2)

hood

center line

h dress for Mini Hana Hood (x 1)

I center line

h hood for Mini Hana Hood (x 1)

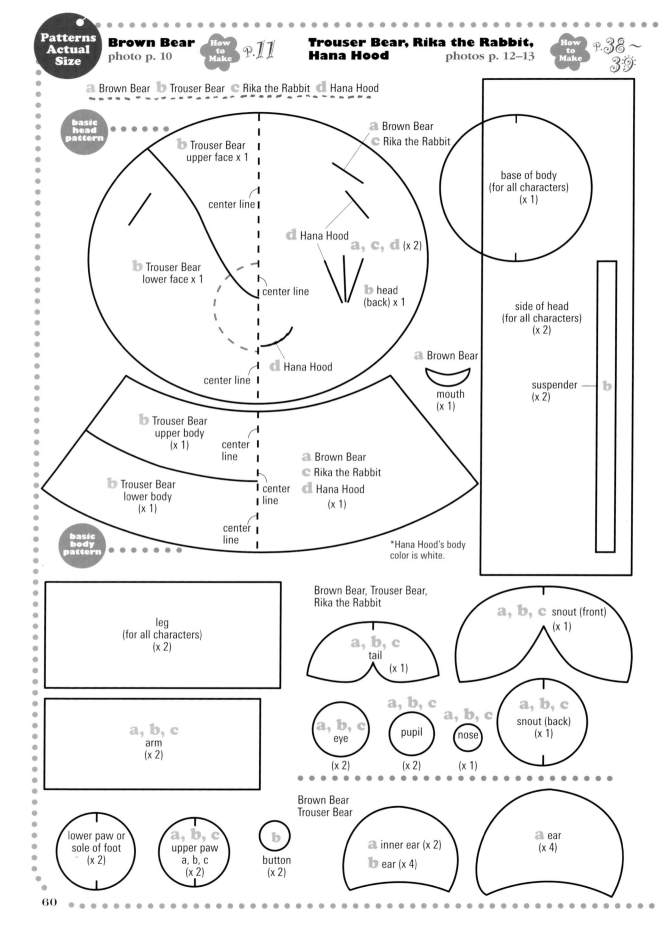

a Brown Bear **b** Trouser Bear **c** Rika the Rabbit **d** Hana Hood

basic head pattern

b Trouser Bear upper face x 1

center line

b Trouser Bear lower face x 1

center line

center line

a Brown Bear
c Rika the Rabbit

d Hana Hood

a, c, d (x 2)

b head (back) x 1

d Hana Hood

a Brown Bear

mouth (x 1)

base of body (for all characters) (x 1)

side of head (for all characters) (x 2)

suspender (x 2) **b**

b Trouser Bear upper body (x 1)

center line

b Trouser Bear lower body (x 1)

center line

center line

a Brown Bear
c Rika the Rabbit
d Hana Hood
(x 1)

basic body pattern

*Hana Hood's body color is white.

leg (for all characters) (x 2)

a, b, c arm (x 2)

Brown Bear, Trouser Bear, Rika the Rabbit

a, b, c tail (x 1)

a, b, c snout (front) (x 1)

a, b, c eye (x 2)

a, b, c pupil (x 2)

a, b, c nose (x 1)

a, b, c snout (back) (x 1)

lower paw or sole of foot (x 2)

a, b, c upper paw a, b, c (x 2)

b button (x 2)

Brown Bear Trouser Bear

a inner ear (x 2)

b ear (x 4)

a ear (x 4)

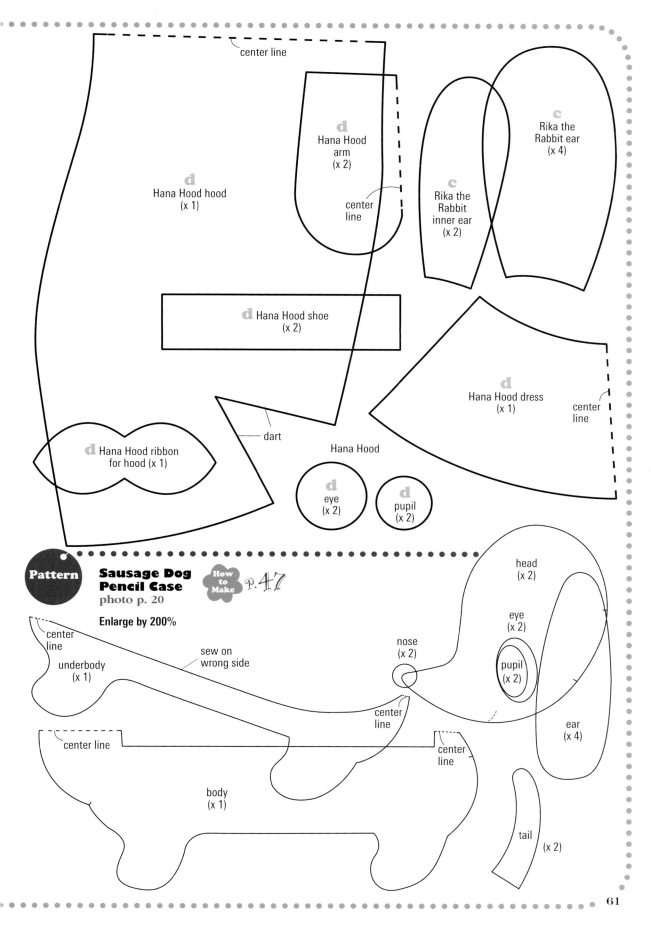

center line

d
Hana Hood hood
(x 1)

d
Hana Hood
arm
(x 2)

center
line

c
Rika the
Rabbit ear
(x 4)

c
Rika the
Rabbit
inner ear
(x 2)

d Hana Hood shoe
(x 2)

d
Hana Hood dress
(x 1)

center
line

dart

d Hana Hood ribbon
for hood (x 1)

Hana Hood

d
eye
(x 2)

d
pupil
(x 2)

Pattern **Sausage Dog Pencil Case** How to Make P.47
photo p. 20

Enlarge by 200%

center
line

underbody
(x 1)

sew on
wrong side

nose
(x 2)

head
(x 2)

eye
(x 2)

pupil
(x 2)

center
line

center line

center
line

ear
(x 4)

body
(x 1)

tail
(x 2)

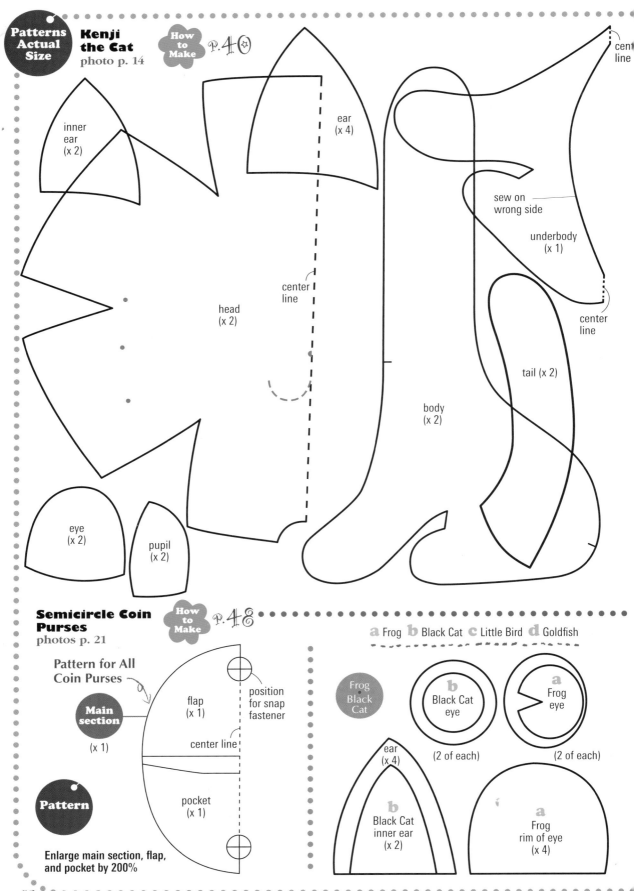

Kenji
the Cat
photo p. 14

How
to
Make P.40

inner
ear
(x 2)

ear
(x 4)

center
line

sew on
wrong side

underbody
(x 1)

head
(x 2)

center
line

center
line

tail (x 2)

body
(x 2)

eye
(x 2)

pupil
(x 2)

Semicircle Coin
Purses
photos p. 21

How
to
Make P.48

a Frog b Black Cat c Little Bird d Goldfish

Pattern for All
Coin Purses

Main
section

(x 1)

flap
(x 1)

position
for snap
fastener

center line

pocket
(x 1)

Pattern

Enlarge main section, flap,
and pocket by 200%

Frog
Black
Cat

b
Black Cat
eye

a
Frog
eye

(2 of each)

(2 of each)

ear
(x 4)

b
Black Cat
inner ear
(x 2)

a
Frog
rim of eye
(x 4)

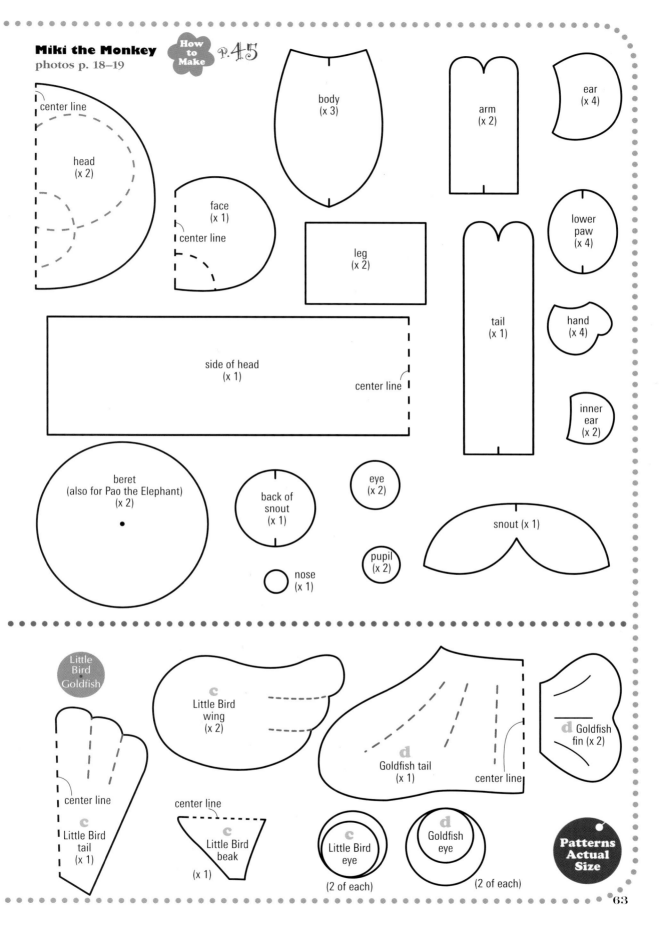

Miki the Monkey
photos p. 18–19

How to Make P.45

center line

head
(x 2)

face
(x 1)
center line

body
(x 3)

arm
(x 2)

ear
(x 4)

lower
paw
(x 4)

leg
(x 2)

tail
(x 1)

hand
(x 4)

side of head
(x 1)
center line

inner
ear
(x 2)

beret
(also for Pao the Elephant)
(x 2)

back of
snout
(x 1)

eye
(x 2)

pupil
(x 2)

snout (x 1)

nose
(x 1)

Little
Bird
•
Goldfish

c
Little Bird wing
(x 2)

d
Goldfish tail
(x 1)
center line

d Goldfish
fin (x 2)

center line

c
Little Bird
tail
(x 1)

center line

c
Little Bird
beak

(x 1)

c
Little Bird
eye

(2 of each)

d
Goldfish
eye

(2 of each)

Patterns
Actual
Size

Afterword

I did my best to make the characters and accessories in this book as cute as can be. It was hard work, with lots of revisions and corrections, but I loved every minute. It made me realize again how much fun it is to make things by hand. I hope you will have a go at making something from this book—it may take you a day, several days, several months, or several years, it doesn't matter. Just take one stitch at a time and discover the pleasure of creating. Finally, thank you from the bottom of my heart for buying this book.

NAOMI TABATHA

Born 1963, Aichi Prefecture, Japan. After working at two toy manufacturers, she began working freelance as a 3D figure illustrator. Her original stuffed toys have graced countless magazine, book, and CD covers. She also creates baby goods and writes columns in women's magazines on making cute stuff. An Aquarius with blood type B, her love of making things by hand is part of the eco-friendly lifestyle she tries to lead.

Originally published by Sekaibunka-sha, Tokyo, in 2009.
Jacket design and layout by Reiko Takechi.
Photography by Tomoyasu Naruse.

Published by Kodansha USA, Inc.
451 Park Avenue South
New York, NY 10016

Distributed in the United Kingdom and continental Europe by Kodansha Europe Ltd.

Copyright © 2010, 2012 by Naomi Tabatha.

All rights reserved. Printed in the United States of America.

ISBN 978-1-56836-387-5

First published in Japan in 2010 by Kodansha International
First US edition 2012 published by Kodansha USA

18 17 16 15 14 13 12   10 9 8 7 6 5 4 3 2 1

The Library of Congress has cataloged the earlier printing as follows:

Library of Congress Cataloging-in-Publication Data

Tabatha, Naomi, 1963-
[Kawaii feruto no komonotachi. English]
Felt friends from Japan : 86 super-cute toys and accessories to make yourself / Naomi Tabatha. -- 1st ed.
    p. cm.
 ISBN 978-4-7700-3141-9
1. Felt work. 2. Soft toys. I. Title.
TT849.5.T3313 2010
746'.0463--dc22

2010033127

www.kodanshausa.com

Thank you ♥

See you